Machines That Travel

Focus: Information

PETER SLOAN &
SHERYL SLOAN

A submarine
travels underwater.

A jet plane travels
in the sky.

A space shuttle
travels into space.

A train travels
on land.

A ship travels
on the sea.

A bus travels
on the road.

A ferry travels
on the water.